THE CHICAGO BLACK SOX TRIAL

A Primary Source Account

Wayne Anderson

rosen central
Primary Source™

The Rosen Publishing Group, Inc., New York

For Gerald, with whom I saw Field of Dreams *on our first date, and for my siblings, Denise, Mark, Marsha, Everold, and Kevin*

Published in 2004 by The Rosen Publishing Group, Inc.
29 East 21st Street, New York, NY 10010

Library of Congress Cataloging-in-Publication Data

Anderson, Wayne, 1966–
The Chicago Black Sox trial: a primary source account/by Wayne Anderson.—1st ed.
    p. cm.—(Great trials of the 20th century)
Includes bibliographical references and index.
ISBN 0-8239-3969-3 (libr. binding)
1. Chicago White Sox (Baseball team—Trials, litigation, etc.)
2. Trials (Conspiracy)—Illinois—Chicago. 3. Baseball—Corrupt practices—United States—History. 4. Baseball—Betting—United States—History.
I. Title. II. Series.
KF224.B57 A53 2003
796.357'64'0977311—dc21

2002153670

Manufactured in the United States of America

Unless otherwise attributed, all quotes in this book are excerpted from court transcripts.

CONTENTS

This photo, taken on October 1, 1919, shows the crowd waiting to get into Redland Field for the opening game of the World Series between the Cincinnati Reds and the Chicago White Sox. Scalpers made a killing that day as approximately 150,000 fans tried to get one of the 33,000 seats available.

INTRODUCTION

The 1919 baseball season was successful and exciting. World War I had just ended, and Americans were eager for their lives to return to normal. To the delight of baseball team owners, fans poured into stadiums in droves. Attendance increased to 6.5 million fans from 3 million in 1918. That year, U.S. soldiers, including 247 professional baseball players, had still been in the trenches in Europe fighting the Great War. It was a time when baseball was America's biggest form of entertainment.

But the dramas on the baseball field were even more impressive than the draw at the gates. Returning fans cheered two thrilling pennant races that lasted until the closing weeks of the season. Many important records were set in 1919: pitcher Walter Johnson threw his fifth career opening-day shutout, Babe Ruth hit twenty-nine home runs, Ty Cobb won his twelfth batting title with an average of .384, and Fred Luderus maintained a 479 consecutive-game streak.

The fans in Chicago seemed to have the most to cheer about. The White Sox were then considered to be the greatest baseball team ever assembled. True to their reputation, the Chicago White Sox won the

1919 American League pennant. They were widely expected to easily beat the Cincinnati Reds in the World Series championship. Eliot Asinof writes in *Eight Men Out*, "It was said that Chicago fans did not come to see them win: they came to see how."

But the mighty Chicago team lost the series five games to three, a result that stunned White Sox fans. Soon many people began to believe the rumors that had been swirling around Chicago. Even before the first pitch was thrown, there were whispers about several White Sox players who planned to "fix" (cheat by losing intentionally) the World Series. In gambling circles, the odds swung sharply in favor of the Cincinnati Reds just days before the start of the series.

The rumors continued well into the 1920 season, toward the end of which they exploded into one of the biggest scandals in American sports history. In the following year, the story became a well-known court case. Eight White Sox players and several gamblers faced charges for conspiring to defraud the public by fixing the 1919 World Series.

Although the Black Sox trial, as the case would come to be known, was a big deal to the public, it was hardly a shining example of the United States's legal system at work. It left many issues unattended and many questions unanswered. However, as part of the larger scandal, the Black Sox trial has had a lasting impact on the game of baseball and sports in general. Oddly enough, the trial that sought to punish the alleged conspirators for "throwing" the World Series appears to have been fixed as well.

THE FIX

Although fifteen people faced charges relating to the World Series fix at one time or another, the main targets were eight White Sox players. These were not ordinary players. Most were stars of the White Sox ball club who ranked among the finest players in the sport. That they conspired to play crooked ball during the World Series was too much for baseball fans to bear.

By all accounts, first baseman Arnold "Chick" Gandil was the ringleader of the group. A roughhouse character, he ran away from home when he was seventeen years old to play "desert ball" in the Arizona border towns near Mexico and to box as a heavyweight fighter. Over the years, Gandil had developed into one of the finest first basemen in baseball. Although he was past his prime in 1919, he continued to hit well and had the best fielding percentage among major league first basemen.

Sometime during the summer of 1919, Gandil hatched a plan to throw the World Series for money. He was confident that he could persuade a number of his teammates to go along with him. On

GANDIL, CHICAGO AMER.

After an unsuccessful stint with the White Sox in 1910, Chick Gandil was reacquired by the team in 1917 to complete Charles Comiskey's dream team. He turned out to be Comiskey's worst nightmare, as his money-making scheme led to the unraveling of one of the best teams in baseball. The photograph on the left shows Gandil in court in June 1921. His baseball card dates from 1909–1911 and was issued by the American Tobacco Company. It is now part of the Benjamin K. Edwards Collection, housed in the Library of Congress.

September 18, two weeks before the start of the series, he approached a bookie named Joseph "Sport" Sullivan and offered him the chance to cash in on the fix. In return, Gandil demanded $80,000 in cash for himself and the players who would participate in the scheme. Sullivan was interested. He promised Gandil he would consider it.

BUILDING THE TEAM

On the following day, Gandil began recruiting his teammates. He approached pitcher Eddie Cicotte first because it was likely that Cicotte would pitch in three of the nine games of the World Series, and Gandil needed pitchers to help secure the fix. Eddie Cicotte had the stuff that scouts raved about and hitters regarded with apprehension. His twenty-nine wins in 1919 led the major leagues, as did his thirty complete games. He had excellent control in the strike zone, a talent that would make his "errors" in the World Series particularly suspicious.

Gandil knew that Cicotte was experiencing difficulties meeting the mortgage payments on a farm that he had recently bought. But the fix was no easy sell. At first, Cicotte rejected Gandil's offers. He later agreed on the condition that he be paid $10,000 before the start of the series.

Eddie Cicotte, pictured here in uniform in this September 18, 1919, photograph, was one of the most pivotal White Sox players in the fixing of the World Series. With Cicotte aboard, Chick Gandil was able to convince other players to participate in the fix.

Gandil next approached his close pal Charles "Swede" Risberg, who was eager to participate. An aggressive player, Risberg played shortstop for the White Sox. He had spectacular range in the field and a strong throwing arm.

Infielder Fred McMullin, who overheard the conversation, demanded to be included. Although not a star athlete—and certainly

This montage of the eight Black Sox players was published in several newspapers in 1920 after the scandal broke. It mocks a 1919 White Sox promotional poster that boasted the full roster of arguably the most talented team in baseball history.

not necessary for the fix—McMullin was a valuable member of the club who could play several positions.

With a little guile and the lure of easy money, Gandil enlisted Joe Jackson, who was the big bat in the White Sox lineup and one of the most feared hitters in baseball. By September 20, Gandil had also gotten commitments from Claude "Lefty" Williams, the team's number two starting pitcher; Charles "Buck" Weaver, arguably the best third baseman in the league; and speedy center fielder Oscar "Happy" Felsch, who was quickly developing into one of the game's most powerful hitters.

Gandil held a meeting of the eight players in his room at the Ansonia Hotel in New York City on September 21. Gandil explained the proposal he had made to Sport Sullivan, and some of the players joked about the mistakes they could fake.

The group that met in that hotel room on that fateful Sunday evening represented the heart of the Chicago White Sox. It included its two best pitchers, three of its four best hitters, two-thirds of the starting outfielders, three-quarters of the starting infielders, and the utility infielder most likely to relieve any of the infielders who needed a break. Collectively, the eight players accounted for 59 percent of the team's wins, 66 percent of the RBIs (runs batted in), 58 percent of the hits, 80 percent of the home runs, and 56 percent of the stolen bases. There is no doubt that, by acting together, they could have blown the series.

The men were also fierce competitors who loved to win and who enjoyed playing baseball. Why, then, would they conspire to lose the World Series? The obvious answer is money. Yet the lure of gamblers' purses may not have been so tempting had the players been satisfied with their baseball salaries. White Sox owner Charles Comiskey, who had spent extravagantly to build an impressive ballpark, court favorable press, and acquire the contracts of his star players from other teams, was downright stingy when it came to paying his players.

SHOELESS JOE JACKSON

Shoeless Joe Jackson was one of Chicago's most celebrated stars. He is considered by many baseball historians to be the greatest natural hitter of his time, possibly of all time.

Once an illiterate millhand from South Carolina, Jackson became a baseball legend long before he made it to the big leagues. He earned the nickname "Shoeless Joe" after performing spectacularly in a game in which he played in his stockings because his new shoes were too tight.

Jackson joined the White Sox in 1915 and terrorized opposing pitchers with his bat, which he named Black Betsy. In the outfield, he possessed an arm like a cannon. In 1919, at age thirty-two, he was at the peak of his career and already boasted statistics that would have made him a shoo-in for the Hall of Fame.

Joe Jackson, Buck Weaver, and Eddie Cicotte were paid an annual salary of $6,000; Chick Gandil and Oscar Felsch earned $4,000; and Claude Williams, Swede Risberg, and Fred McMullin received less than $3,000. According to Asinof, "Compared with their 1919 World Series rivals from Cincinnati, these figures were pitiful . . . Many second-rate ballplayers on second-division ball clubs made more than the White Sox."

There was little that the players could do about their salaries. At the time, major league contracts included a reserve clause that bound each player for his entire career to the club that first brought him to the major leagues. If a player refused to accept the terms of the contract that a team offered him, he could not play for any other professional team.

BANKROLLING THE FIX

Gandil met with Sullivan the morning after the meeting to finalize the deal. He demanded to be paid before the start of the series. Somehow, word of the players' intentions reached another gambler, Bill Burns, who contacted Eddie Cicotte and proposed a competing offer. Cicotte arranged a meeting between himself, Gandil, Burns, and Burns's associate, Billy Maharg. In the meeting, Gandil offered Burns the fix for $100,000 to be paid in cash in advance of the series.

Neither Burns nor Sport Sullivan could come up with the money on his own on such short notice. Separately, each sought the financial backing of Arnold Rothstein, an infamous gambler and sportsman who was known in gambling circles as "the Big Bankroll."

Burns approached Rothstein first, and through his right-hand man, Abe Attell, Rothstein turned him down. However, Attell recognized an opportunity to cash in on the fix for himself. Lying to Burns, Attell told him that Rothstein had changed his mind but did not want his involvement to be known.

Sport Sullivan contacted Arnold Rothstein on September 26 about his own plan for the fix. This time, Rothstein was interested, in part because he had a good opinion of Sullivan. Rothstein sent Nat Evans, an associate, to Chicago with Sullivan to find out whether the players were really serious about selling out the series. He instructed Evans to use the alias Rachael Brown as a cover, in case the operation should go awry.

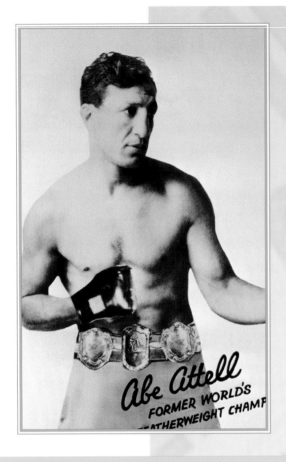 

This publicity handout *(left)* shows Abe Attell during his glory days as the world's featherweight boxing champion, a title he held for twelve years, ending in 1912. Of his 365 professional fights, he lost only six, and those he lost were widely regarded as having been thrown. He met famed gambler Arnold Rothstein *(right)* in 1905 and became his right-hand man after he retired from the ring. Attell double-crossed Rothstein to cash in on the World Series fix.

THE GAMBLERS CHANGE THE RULES

Rothstein had already decided to back the fix by the time Evans approved the plan. He instructed Evans to give Sullivan $40,000 to take care of the players. Rothstein arranged to have the other $40,000 placed in a safe at the Congress Hotel in Chicago, to be paid to the players if the White Sox lost the series. He also requested that Cicotte hit the first Cincinnati batter he faced, as a signal that the fix was on.

Instead of paying the players, Sullivan used $29,000 of the money Evans gave him to bet on the Cincinnati Reds. When he met with Gandil to turn over a paltry $10,000, Gandil was furious. In the end, Gandil had little choice but to accept the money. He left the $10,000 under a pillow in Cicotte's room. Upon finding it, Cicotte sewed the money into the lining of one of his jackets.

Attell also decided to change the payment arrangement. In a meeting with the players on October 1, he announced that he would pay them $20,000 after each loss. The players objected at first, but finally they gave in. They also committed to losing the first three games.

Hugh Fullerton, a syndicated sportswriter from the *Chicago Herald-Examiner*, was bothered by all the buzz about a fix circulating in the hotel where the White Sox players were booked for their trip to Cincinnati. He was shocked by how quickly the gambling odds had turned in favor of the Reds. Dismayed, he sent out a wire to all the newspapers that were to pick up his coverage of the game. It read, "Advise all not to bet on this series. Ugly rumors afloat."

THE SERIES

Half an hour before the start of game 1, Redland Field, the Reds' home stadium, was packed with excited fans. In the Cincinnati dugout, Reds manager Pat Moran gave his team a pep talk, reassuring them that the White Sox could be beaten. He demanded the same fighting spirit that had won the Reds the National League pennant.

The scene in the opposing dugout was strikingly different. When White Sox manager Kid Gleason addressed the rumors of a fix in his pregame meeting, his words were met with shocked stares from some players and hung heads from others. The manager's faith in his club must have been further shaken when a sulking Joe Jackson told him that he felt ill and did not want to play. Gleason dismissed Jackson's excuse and ordered him to play.

GAME 1

In the bottom of the first inning, Cicotte hit Maurice Rath, the Reds' leadoff batter, with his second pitch, signaling that the fix was on. Cicotte was pulled from the game in the bottom of the fourth inning when he gave up five runs. The White Sox eventually lost the game, 9–1. Hugh Fullerton noted one suspicious play and questioned several others.

Kid Gleason was seething after the game. He didn't like what he had seen on the field. He felt that his ballplayers—Cicotte in particular—had not given their best efforts. Later that evening, the manager met with Charles Comiskey to discuss the rumors of a fix. He told Comiskey that he didn't have any proof but that he strongly believed that something was wrong. Convinced, Comiskey took his concerns to American League president Ban Johnson, who accused him of being a sore loser.

For the loss, the players received no payment. When they complained, Attell showed them a telegram that appeared to have been sent by Arnold Rothstein. The telegram stated that the team would be paid the following morning. The truth was that the telegram was a fake. Attell had arranged for a friend in New York to send it so that he could trick the players.

An enraged Kid Gleason confronted Eddie Cicotte in the lobby of the Hotel Sinton in Cincinnati, Ohio, after the game 1 loss on October 1, 1919, and openly accused the pitcher of throwing the game. He is pictured here in a promotional White Sox photograph, taken on the field sometime between 1919 and 1923.

GAME 2

Before the start of game 2, Gleason instructed White Sox catcher Ray

Schalk to pay close attention to the way Lefty Williams pitched. To most observers, Williams pitched a good game, despite losing 4–2. He had demonstrated the pinpoint control that fans expected of him. But Schalk was not fooled. After the game, the fiery catcher complained to Gleason that Williams kept crossing him up (throwing unexpected pitches), especially in the fourth inning. He

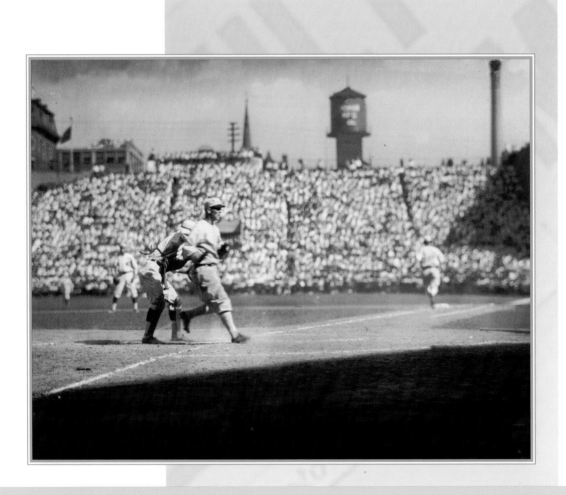

Buck Weaver is tagged out at the plate during game 2 of the 1919 World Series on October 2 at Redland Field in Cincinnati, Ohio. By most accounts, Weaver played honestly and with his usual hustle during the series even though he had earlier agreed to participate in the fix. This photograph is now housed in the Chicago Historical Society.

demanded that Gleason do something about the crooked play and later physically attacked Williams before leaving the stadium.

When Burns went to Attell's room to collect the $40,000 now owed to the players for two losses, he saw a room full of money. But Attell gave him only $10,000. Burns gave this money to Gandil, who made a fuss about being double-crossed. Meanwhile, the other gambler, Sport Sullivan, was nowhere to be found.

GAME 3

Before game 3, which was played in Chicago on October 3, Gandil told Burns that the White Sox would also lose that game. Burns, in turn, wagered everything he had won on games 1 and 2 on the Cincinnati Reds. But with their teammate Dickie Kerr pitching a three-hit, complete-game shutout, the conspirators couldn't prevent the White Sox from winning the game. The Sox won 3–0, with Chick Gandil driving in two of the three runs.

This victory didn't make Burns a happy man, for he lost all his money betting on the wrong team. Then, he went to collect more money from Attell, who told him he wouldn't give the players any more money until after the next loss. This time around, Gandil refused to go along. He told the gambler that without more money the fix was off. To add insult to injury, Burns asked for a 10 percent commission on the $10,000 he had already secured for the players. Gandil refused. Beaten, Burns told Attell that the fix was over.

But the fix was still alive. The following morning, October 4, Gandil spoke with Sport Sullivan and threatened to call off the fix if he didn't get payments of $20,000 before games 4 and 5. Sullivan scrambled to send Gandil $20,000 that morning and reminded the player of the $40,000 already in the safe at the Congress Hotel.

GAME 4

Cicotte pitched well in game 4, but, again, he had one bad inning. This time, it was the fifth, when he made two fielding errors that resulted in Cincinnati runs. Hugh Fullerton circled the errors on his scorecard as being suspicious. The White Sox lost the game 2–0.

After the game, Gandil divided the $20,000 he had received from Sport Sullivan evenly between Felsch, Risberg, Williams, and Jackson. At this point, six of the eight players, including Gandil, had received some money. Gandil decided that McMullin would have to wait until they received more money and that Weaver wouldn't be paid at all because the third baseman appeared to have pulled himself out of the deal by playing hard in all the games.

GAME 5

Game 5 was scoreless until the sixth inning, when Lefty Williams surrendered four runs to the Reds. An annoyed Hugh Fullerton noted at least three poor fielding plays—two by Felsch and one by Risberg—that added to Williams's loss of control in the inning. The game ended in a 5–0 victory by the Reds, giving them a four-to-one edge in the series. They needed to win only one more game to become world champions.

THE PLAYERS CALL OFF THE FIX

When Sullivan didn't show up with the other $20,000 before or after game 5, Gandil and several of the White Sox players agreed to call off the fix. With this change of heart, the White Sox, playing as a united team for the first time in the series, won the next two games. At this point, the series stood at four games to three in favor of the Reds.

This 1919 photo gives a partial view of the stands and players on the field during one of the World Series games in Chicago. Despite Comiskey's later claims that the scandal hurt his ticket sales, rumors of a fix may have helped fill the stands.

There was a good chance that the White Sox could even the series in the next game, which was to be played on their home turf.

For Rothstein, the situation was too close for comfort. He told Sullivan to order the players to lose the next game, but Sullivan knew he couldn't count on Gandil to carry out Rothstein's wishes. So he set his sights on Williams, who was slated to pitch game 8. But Sullivan didn't call Williams himself. Instead, he paid a Chicago thug known as Harry F to threaten to harm Williams and his wife if the pitcher didn't lose the next game. Williams was to make sure that game 8 was essentially over in the first inning.

On his way to the press box, Hugh Fullerton ran into a gambler who predicted that the first inning would be the biggest first inning the writer would ever see. And it was. In fifteen pitches, Williams surrendered four runs. With only one out in the inning, Gleason yanked Williams from the game. The White Sox lost the game 10–5. They had lost the series five games to three.

The following day, Sullivan gave Gandil the $40,000 from the hotel safe. From that sum, Gandil paid Risberg $10,000 and McMullin $5,000. For all his complaints about the gamblers not being on the level, Gandil did not treat his fellow players fairly. Of the $80,000 he received for the fix, he pocketed $35,000, while paying Risberg $15,000, Cicotte $10,000, and Jackson, Williams, Felsch, and McMullin each only $5,000.

EXPOSURE

The day after the final game, Joe Jackson took his $5,000 to Comiskey's office hoping to get the load of guilt off his mind. Although Jackson waited for several hours and insisted that his visit was important and personal, Comiskey refused to see him. (Two weeks later, Jackson sent Comiskey a note offering to tell all that he knew about the fix.)

Comiskey was too shaken by his team's loss and the rumors surrounding it to see Jackson. According to Asinof in *Eight Men Out*, in a later meeting with Gleason and Fullerton, Comiskey declared, "There are seven boys who will never play on this team again!" Comiskey's friend and lawyer, Alfred Austrian, persuaded Comiskey that he risked destroying his ball club and losing a lot of money by going after the crooked players. Several days later, Comiskey changed his tune and released a statement to the press that read: "I believe my boys fought the battles of the recent World Series on the level, as they have always done. And I would be the first to want information to the contrary—if there be any. I would give $20,000 to anyone unearthing any information to that effect."

Kid Gleason *(left)* chats with White Sox owner Charles Comiskey during a meeting in Chicago in 1919. The two met several times during and after the 1919 World Series to discuss rumors of crooked ballplayers on the team. Although Gleason was convinced that several players were throwing games, he could not give Comiskey any concrete evidence. This photograph was taken by a *Chicago Daily News* photographer and can be found in the Chicago Historical Society.

Despite Comiskey's efforts, the talk of the fix would not go away. On December 15, 1919, the *New York World* published an article by Hugh Fullerton that suggested that the World Series had been fixed. Fullerton charged that owners routinely sat idly by while players were being bribed and the outcomes of games were sold. Baseball team owners ignored the article, and much of the national media made light of it.

Nevertheless, rumors of the 1919 World Series fix followed the White Sox throughout the 1920 season, and there was additional talk of the White Sox blowing individual games in the new season while engaged in another pennant race. In fact, rumors of blown games throughout the league became rampant.

A GRAND JURY INVESTIGATES

One of these rumors led to the convening of a grand jury in Cook County, Illinois. A grand jury is a group that is assembled to examine evidence to determine if someone should be charged with a crime. On September 24, New York Giants pitcher Rube Benton told the grand jury that he had seen a telegram regarding the 1919 World Series fix. He named Gandil, Cicotte, Felsch, and Williams as having been involved. The following day, the foreman of the grand jury revealed to the press the names of a number of gamblers, including Rothstein, Burns, and Attell, who were also implicated in the scheme.

The media drummed up these revelations into a whirlwind of scandal. On September 27, the Philadelphia *North American* published a tell-all interview with gambler Billy Maharg, who gave an account of his involvement in the fix.

Following these revelations, the grand jury subpoenaed Comiskey to tell what he knew. Comiskey testified that he had investigated rumors about game fixing but did not find any solid evidence that he could use against the players.

THE CONFESSIONS

Finally, the weight of the scandal became too much for Cicotte to bear. It became obvious to the people around him that something was troubling him. So when Kid Gleason suggested that he come clean with whatever was bothering him, the pitcher willingly attended a meeting with Gleason,

Out of his hatred for Charles Comiskey and his desire to weaken the White Sox ball club, Ban Johnson *(right)*, president of the American League, worked hard to stoke the grand jury investigation. He even hired a private investigator to tail Eddie Cicotte, which was one of the reasons for the pitcher's unease in the weeks before his confession. Johnson would go on to assist in the criminal prosecution of the Black Sox players. He is pictured here during a January 25, 1915, meeting with Pennsylvania governor John Tener *(left)* and Garry Herrman, president of the National League.

Comiskey, and Austrian, Comiskey's lawyer. When Cicotte began to confess, Comiskey ordered him to tell it to the grand jury. Austrian then led Cicotte to the Cook County Courthouse, where he coaxed the pitcher into appearing before the grand jury without legal representation and signing a waiver of immunity (a legal document giving up a witness's right not to have his or her grand jury testimony used against him or her as the basis for prosecution) by telling him that he had nothing to worry about.

Before the grand jury, Cicotte made a tearful and guilt-ridden confession that lasted for more than two hours. He explained how he had been drawn into the scheme, naming all the participants as he went on. Still, Judge Charles McDonald was dissatisfied with the testimony because Cicotte couldn't deliver concrete evidence of Arnold Rothstein's involvement.

When Joe Jackson received word of Cicotte's confession, he decided that he, too, wanted to talk. As he had done with Cicotte, Austrian tricked Jackson into signing away his immunity before testifying to the grand jury without the counsel of a lawyer. Through it all, Jackson seemed intent on establishing three things: He had been given only a portion of the money that he was promised; he played to win; and he was ashamed of his involvement in the fix.

This 1920 photograph shows Joe Jackson being questioned on the witness stand by state's attorney Hartley Repogle. Legend has it that when Jackson exited the courtroom, a young boy looked at his fallen hero and begged, "Say it ain't so, Joe. Say it ain't so."

Shortly after Jackson's testimony, Comiskey dispatched telegrams to the eight suspected players, suspending them from the team.

Having received his notice of suspension and after talking things over with his wife and with Jackson, Lefty Williams decided that he, too, should confess. His would be the third and final grand jury confession. Unlike Jackson and Cicotte, Williams did not appear before the grand jury. Instead, he signed a sworn statement in which he answered questions posed by Austrian. He, too, signed a waiver of immunity. He did not mention his encounter with the gangster Harry F before game 8.

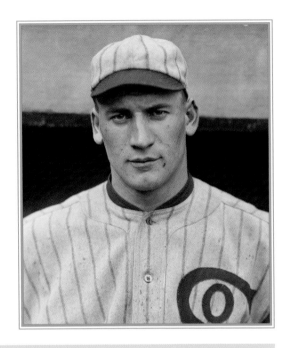

This portrait of Oscar "Happy" Felsch was taken on October 29, 1917. Felsch enjoyed a great season in 1920, hitting .338 with 188 hits and 14 home runs. But he knew his career was over when news of the Black Sox scandal broke.

Harry Reutlinger, a reporter for the *Chicago American*, tracked down Happy Felsch at Chicago's Warner Hotel and, with a bottle of whiskey, convinced the ballplayer to tell his version of the story. Felsch confirmed Cicotte's account of the fix and admitted that he had agreed to participate in the plot because he didn't want to be left out of making money on a deal that possibly would have gone on without him. He accepted responsibility for being involved in the fix, although he insisted that he didn't commit any crooked plays, mostly because of the lack of opportunity. His regret was real, and he firmly grasped the irony of his situation when he told the reporter, "I got five thousand dollars. I could have got just about that much for being on the level if the Sox had won the Series. And now I'm out of baseball—the only profession I knew anything about—and a lot of gamblers have gotten rich. The joke seems to be on us."

A SURPRISE GRAND JURY TESTIMONY

The grand jury was interested in hearing from gamblers Attell and Sullivan, but Rothstein's attorney, William Fallon, made sure that these men were out of the reach of grand jury subpoenas by having his client pay them to leave the country. With these witnesses out of the way, Fallon convinced Rothstein to appear before the Cook County grand jury. Rothstein told the grand jury that he had chosen to appear because he was annoyed by all the suggestions that he had been involved in the fix and that he wanted to set the record straight. He read a prepared statement in which he blamed Abe Attell for the fix. He said, "I don't doubt that Attell used my name to put it over. That's been done by smarter men than Abe. But I wasn't in on it, wouldn't have gone into it under any circumstances, and didn't bet a cent on the series after I found out what was under way." After asking Rothstein a few easy questions, the grand jury decided that he had not been involved.

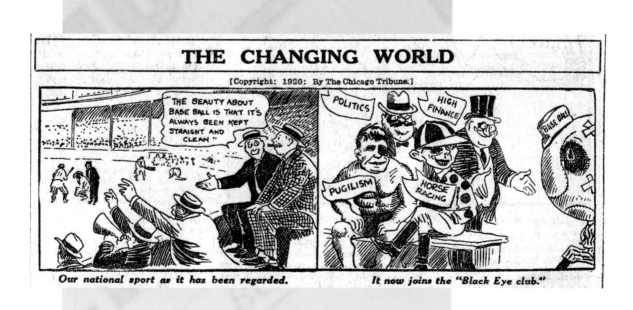

The ill-repute into which organized baseball fell in the wake of the Black Sox scandal is captured in this two-paneled newspaper cartoon from *The Chicago Tribune* of September 24, 1920. Drawn by artist John McCutcheon, it shows a black-eyed baseball in the company of boxing, horse racing, politics, and high finance, areas long considered to be riddled with corruption.

INDICTMENTS

By the time the grand jury wrapped up its investigation, it had heard from a number of witnesses. On October 22, 1920, the grand jury indicted, or legally accused, the eight Chicago players and five gamblers—Attell, Burns, Sullivan, Rachael Brown (Nat Evans), and former White Sox pitcher Hal Chase—on nine counts of conspiracy to defraud various individuals and organizations in the state of Illinois.

REACTION TO THE SCANDAL

Major league owners appointed Judge Kenesaw Mountain Landis baseball commissioner in 1920 to signal their willingness to clean up the sport. An avid baseball fan, Landis enjoyed national esteem for his honesty and integrity.

From this point onward, the eight players would be referred to as the Black Sox. The front pages of newspapers all across the United States carried photographs of the eight players, presenting them as the country's latest villains—the boys who sullied the game. Asinof reports that cynicism about baseball ran so rampant in Chicago that little children who once idolized ballplayers were shouting "play bail" instead of "play ball" in the city streets. The national pastime was in trouble and on trial.

In response to the mushrooming scandal, team owners decided to create the position of commissioner of baseball, a post that would carry sweeping powers to rule on issues in both leagues, including disciplinary actions against owners. The man

Judge Kenesaw Mountain Landis *(seated)* meets with major league owners in a courtroom in Chicago, Illinois, soon after his appointment as baseball commissioner in 1920. From left to right, the owners are: Robert Quinn (St. Louis Browns), William Veeck (Chicago Cubs), Harry Frazee (Boston Red Sox), August Herrmann (Cincinnati Reds), Charles Stoneham (New York Giants), James Dunn (Cleveland Indians), Charles Ebbets (Brooklyn Dodgers), Sam Breadon (St. Louis Cardinals), Jacob Ruppert (New York Yankees), Frank Navin (Detroit Tigers), Clark Griffith (Washington Senators), Barney Dreyfuss (Pittsburgh Pirates), Phil Ball (St. Louis Browns), and Connie Mack (Philadelphia Athletics). This photo was taken by a *Chicago Daily News* photographer and is now housed in the Chicago Historical Society.

they chose to fill this role was Kenesaw Mountain Landis, a fiery, no-nonsense judge who was widely respected as a man of integrity. As baseball's commissioner, Landis would also sit in judgment of the Black Sox. While a Cook County trial jury would decide whether the players would be fined or imprisoned for their role in the World Series fix, Landis would decide their fate in professional baseball.

PRETRIAL MANEUVERS

The indictment of the players and gamblers meant that they would have to face a criminal trial. A trial jury would decide whether the charges in the indictment were true. If the thirteen defendants were found guilty, they could be fined or imprisoned.

The American criminal justice system pits two sides against each other. It balances the rights of defendants, those people charged with committing a crime, with the interest of the prosecution, which acts on behalf of the people of the state (or the country, if the federal government is the accuser). Accordingly, the names of criminal trials generally reflect this relationship between the state and the defendants. Thus the Black Sox trial was officially known as the *People of the State of Illinois v. Edward V. Cicotte, et al.*

In criminal cases, the prosecution has the burden of proof. This means that the defendant is presumed to be innocent. Then the prosecution has to prove, beyond a reasonable doubt, that the defendant committed the crime or crimes stated in the indictment. If the defense feels that the prosecution has not proven its charges, it may choose not to present any evidence.

CHALLENGES OF THE PROSECUTION

The task of bringing the Black Sox players and their gambling associates to trial was assigned to an assistant state's attorney named George Gorman. Gorman was not eager to bring the case to trial after he reviewed the charges and the evidence. He thought that the charges in the indictments were confusing and difficult to prove, and that witnesses would be hard to track down. He also noted that much of the baseball establishment, with the exception of American League president Ban Johnson, was opposed to the trial.

One fact stood above the others in explaining Gorman's reluctance:

This 1964 photograph, taken by Harold Allen, shows Chicago's historic Criminal Courts Building. Both the grand jury proceedings and the Black Sox trial took place in this building.

Someone had stolen the waivers of immunity and the players' signed confessions. Reportedly, Austrian and Fallon, the lawyers for Comiskey and Rothstein respectively, had arranged for the outgoing state attorney, who had recently lost his bid for reelection, to remove these documents before leaving his position. Notwithstanding these setbacks, Gorman, at the prodding of Ban Johnson, who offered to work closely with the prosecution, set the wheels of the trial in motion.

A FALSE START

On February 14, 1921, an arraignment was held in the Chicago Criminal Courts Building. Gorman

This photograph, published in the *Chicago Daily News* in 1921, captures six of the accused White Sox players with their attorneys. Seated from left to right are Chick Gandil, Claude Williams, Charles Risberg, Eddie Cicotte, Buck Weaver, Joe Jackson, and attorney Thomas Nash. Attorneys James O'Brien and Max Luster and two unidentified men stand in the background.

and the presiding judge, William Dever, were stunned to see the team of defense lawyers. It included not only some of the most prominent high-priced lawyers in Illinois but also former assistant state's attorney Henry Berger. Worse was the inclusion of James O'Brien, who only weeks before had worked with Gorman to develop the prosecution's case.

THE STAGES OF A CRIMINAL TRIAL

- **Arraignment** The stage at the beginning of a trial in which the accused person or persons are called before a court to answer the charges made against them—that is, to plead guilty or not guilty.
- **Jury Selection**
- **Opening Statements** Each side outlines the case and evidence that it intends to present to the jury.
- **Presentation of the Prosecution's Witnesses**
    - -Direct Examination: The questioning of a witness by the party that calls him or her
    - -Cross-Examination: The questioning of a witness by the opposing party
- **Presentation of the Defense's Witnesses**
    - -Direct Examination
    - -Cross-Examination
- **Closing Arguments** Each side summarizes the arguments it has made during the trial and tries to show why the arguments of the opposing party should be rejected.
- **Judge's Instruction to the Jury** The judge explains to the jury how to apply the law to the facts that were presented in the trial.
- **Jury Deliberation** The jury meets in private to determine whether or not the defendants are guilty.
- **Reading of the Verdict**

Judge William Dever sits in a Chicago courtroom in this *Chicago Daily News* photograph taken in 1920. The photograph is now housed in the Chicago Historical Society. Dever presided over the arraignment and pretrial proceedings but was not involved in the final trial.

The defense lawyers immediately petitioned for, or formally requested, a bill of particulars. A bill of particulars is a statement that clearly itemizes the charges in greater detail than the list of charges set forth in the indictments. In a later session, Judge Dever ordered the state to provide a bill of particulars to the defense by March 1, a mere two weeks away. In response to this order, Gorman announced that the players' confessions had been stolen and that he needed more time to reconvene the grand jury to prepare new evidence. With this startling revelation, the judge was forced to give the prosecution more time.

A SCRAMBLE FOR WITNESSES

During the time gained by the postponement of the trial, Gorman and his team worked furiously to uncover new evidence and find witnesses. Within a week, his grand jury had handed down several new indictments and spun a new twist on the conspiracy theory. By the end of April, Gorman had issued arrest warrants for the indicted ballplayers and gamblers, and subpoenas for other potential witnesses of whom he had become aware.

Wherever they could, Austrian and Fallon frustrated Gorman's attempts to get evidence by bribing potential witnesses to change their stories or to feign ignorance. However, Ban Johnson came through for Gorman when he tracked down Bill Burns in Del Rio, Texas, and convinced the gambler to testify for the prosecution with the guarantee of immunity.

With this witness, the prosecution was ready to begin its case.

THE TRIAL

The Black Sox trial began on June 27, 1921, to a packed courthouse with Judge Hugo Friend presiding. By then, the charges had been dropped against many of those involved due to a lack of evidence. Only seven of the players and two gamblers (Dave Zelser and Carl Zork, associates of Abe Attell) were being tried. The charges were:

- A conspiracy to defraud the public
- A conspiracy to defraud Ray Schalk
- A conspiracy to commit a confidence game
- A conspiracy to injure the business of the American League
- A conspiracy to injure the business of Charles A. Comiskey

The players' attorneys immediately filed a motion to dismiss the trial, claiming that the charges spelled out in the bill of particulars were not crimes under Illinois law. They may have made this claim because, at the time of the 1919 World Series, there was no law in Illinois that specifically outlawed the fixing of a sporting event. Therefore, they

This portrait of Judge Hugo Friend was taken in his chamber, or office, at the Criminal Courts Building in Chicago, Illinois, on July 22, 1921. Baseball historians regard Judge Friend as having been sympathetic to the Black Sox players. His final instructions to the jury, which were widely criticized in newspaper editorials at the time, are thought to have improperly influenced the verdict.

charged, it was not illegal for the players to play below their abilities. Nevertheless, Judge Friend ruled against the defense a week later and proceeded with jury selection.

THE CASE FOR THE PROSECUTION

While delivering his opening arguments on July 18, George Gorman began quoting from a copy of Cicotte's confession. The defense lawyers immediately objected. Michael Ahearn, who represented Weaver, Risberg, and Felsch, shouted, "You won't get to first base with those confessions." Gorman replied, "We'll hit a home run with them!" Ahearn rallied with, "You may get a long hit, but you'll be thrown out at the plate!" The baseball metaphors were not lost on the packed courtroom audience, who chuckled at the exchange. In the end, the judge ruled the confessions inadmissible.

Charles Comiskey was the first witness called by the prosecution. Gorman walked the White Sox owner through the highlights of his brilliant baseball career during the direct examination. On cross-examination, defense attorney Benedict Short, who represented Jackson, Williams, and Cicotte, attempted to show that Comiskey had made more money in 1920 than he had in any other previous year. Gorman objected to this line of questioning, arguing that Comiskey's finances were irrelevant. When Judge Friend sided with the prosecutor, Short complained, "This man [Comiskey] is getting richer all the time, and my clients are charged with conspiracy to injure his business," before excusing Comiskey from the stand.

Bill Burns was the next prosecution witness, and his testimony would last for several days. Questioned by another assistant state's attorney, Edward Prindeville, Burns recounted his meetings with the players, naming Gandil, McMullin, Williams, Felsch, Cicotte, and Weaver. He also mentioned his contacts with other gamblers

This is a photo of Bill Burns testifying on the witness stand during the Black Sox trial on July 21, 1921. Burns was the primary prosecution witness whose testimony caused some concern for the defense. During cross-examination, Burns admitted that one of the reasons he was testifying was that the players had not given him a cut of the $10,000 he had raised for them.

such as Rothstein, Attell, and a man named Bennett, all of whom he identified as the financiers. He pointed out Cicotte in the courtroom and, when asked if Bennett was in the courtroom, signaled at Zelser. Burns was a convincing witness on the stand, and his confidence seemed to grow the longer he testified. This was even more evident when he was cross-examined by the defense lawyers. He seemed to have a good time meeting their aggressive questioning with his own snappy remarks.

After Burns's testimony, the prosecution again tried to get the jury to hear the grand jury confessions of Cicotte, Jackson, and Williams. Gorman informed the judge that the original documents had disap-

peared from the evidence room but that he had copies of the confessions and a number of witnesses—including grand jurors and court stenographers—who were willing to testify. Judge Friend ruled that he would allow the confessions to be used only if the prosecution could prove that they were made voluntarily. With the waivers of immunity also missing, this would not be an easy task for the prosecution.

For this purpose, Gorman called to the stand Hartley Replogle, the former assistant state's attorney who had questioned Cicotte and Jackson before the grand jury. Replogle testified that the ballplayers had signed the waivers of immunity willingly and without any offer of reward.

Assistant state's attorney George Gorman, pictured here in an unrelated proceeding in 1925, vigorously prosecuted the Black Sox players, even after Judge Friend told him that he would not allow a guilty verdict against them to stand.

Still, Judge Friend was not satisfied. Eventually, he excused the jurors from the courtroom to allow for the confessors to be questioned in private. Cicotte and Jackson admitted to signing something but claimed they didn't know what it was. Gorman later called Judge MacDonald, who had presided over the grand jury and who now testified that the players had not been deprived of their rights.

Judge Friend allowed the confessions into evidence but limited their use to proving the guilt of the three players who had made them. This was a huge victory for the prosecution because, even with Burns's testimony, Gorman realized that he had not achieved the standard of proof beyond a reasonable doubt necessary to secure a conviction. Without the confessions, his case amounted to nothing more than one man's word against another's. But to have the jurors hear how the players had admitted their role in the fix could sway the jury to see things his way.

In his grand jury testimony, Cicotte had said, "Gandil asked me my price . . . and I told him $10,000 to be paid [in cash] in advance."

And on the question of how the games were thrown, he offered:

It's easy. Just a slight hesitation on the player's part will let a man get to base or make a run. I did it by not putting a thing on the ball. You could have read the trade mark on it the way I lobbed it over the plate. A baby could have hit 'em. Schalk was wise the moment I started pitching . . . All the runs scored against me were due to my own deliberate errors. In those two games, I did not try to win.

The prosecution then introduced the portions of Joe Jackson's testimony in which he admitted to being paid to throw the series:

Question: Did anybody pay you any money to help throw that series in favor of Cincinnati?

Answer: They did.

Question: How much did they pay you?

Answer: They promised me $20,000, and paid me five.

Question: Who promised you the twenty thousand?

Answer: Chick Gandil

Question: Who paid you the $5,000?

Answer: Lefty Williams brought it in my room and threw it down.

After reading from the players' confessions, the prosecution rested, or ended its presentation.

THE CASE FOR THE DEFENSE

The defense lawyers called few witnesses, and only one of the defendants, the gambler Zelser, testified. The players' lawyers called Gleason and a number of the active White Sox players to the stand. The prosecution objected every time the defense asked one of these witnesses if he thought that the players on trial had given their best efforts during the series. Each time the judge sustained the objection. The opinions of the so-called clean players would not be heard. It is not clear why the prosecution objected to this line of questioning, but Gorman may have felt that Comiskey, in an effort to protect his reputation and his ball club from further harm, had persuaded his employees to reply that the Black Sox players had given their all.

Finally, the defense called White Sox secretary Harry Grabiner to the stand. Grabiner testified that the ball club's gate receipts increased from $521,175.75 in 1919 to $910,206.59 in 1920.

Although Eddie Cicotte, Joe Jackson, and Claude Williams testifed before the grand jury without the benefit of legal counsel, they were well represented in the criminal trial by Benedict Short (pictured here in a 1928 photo), a former state's attorney and one of Chicago's most prominent and expensive defense lawyers. This photograph was taken by a *Chicago Daily News* photographer and is now housed in the Chicago Historical Society.

Attorney Short made it clear that, given this significant increase in revenue, the defendants could not have ruined the financial health of the White Sox.

CLOSING STATEMENTS

Three lawyers made closing statements for the defense. Benedict Short described the prosecution's case as being weak, declaring that "the state failed to establish criminal conspiracy." He added, "There may have been an agreement entered by the defendants to take the gambler's money, but it has not been shown the players had any intention of defrauding the public or of bringing the game into ill repute."

Morgan Frumberg, who represented the gamblers, made an appeal to the jury's sense of fair play. "Why was [Rothstein] not indicted?" he asked. "Why were these underpaid ballplayers, these penny-ante gamblers from Des Moines and St. Louis, who may have bet a few nickels on the World Series, brought here to be the goats in this case? Ask the powers in baseball. Ask Ban Johnson who pulled the strings in this case."

Michael Ahearn made a more direct attack on Johnson, accusing him of buying evidence to control the case. He also accused Bill Burns of lying because of a bribe from Johnson.

On July 29, Edward Prindeville made the prosecution's closing argument. He appealed to the jurors' emotions and to their love of the game. He asked, "What more convincing proof do you want than the statement made by the ballplayers. Joe Jackson, Eddie Cicotte, and Williams sold out the American public for a paltry $20,000 . . . I say, gentlemen, that the evidence shows that a swindle and a con game has been worked on the American people . . . They went to see a ball game. But all they saw was a con game."

THE VERDICT

Before turning over a case to the jury for deliberation, a judge is required to instruct the jury on how to examine the facts and interpret the law. In the Black Sox trial, Judge Friend told the jury that in order to find the players guilty, the jurors would have to determine that the players had conspired not only to throw the World Series but also to defraud the public and others. An editorial printed in the *New York Times* quipped that the instruction sounded like "asking whether the defendant intended to murder his victim or merely to cut his head off." The judge's instruction seemed like a gift to the defense.

After deliberating for only two hours, the jury came back with "not guilty" verdicts for all the defendants. The scene in the courtroom was one of celebration. Spectators cheered as the acquitted players rushed to thank the jurors. Even Judge Friend was reported to have been smiling and waving at the players.

THE AFTERMATH

Baseball's Commissioner Landis was a harsher judge and jury. The next morning, he released the following statement to the press:

> Regardless of the verdict of juries, no player who throws a ballgame, no player that undertakes or promises to throw a ballgame, no player who sits in conference with a bunch of crooked players and gamblers where the ways and means of throwing a game are discussed and does not promptly tell his club about it, will ever play professional baseball.

The most prominent newspapers in the country ridiculed the jury's verdict as a miscarriage of justice and praised the decision of baseball's new commissioner. But if the reaction of the spectators in the courtroom is any indication, the opinions of the editorial pages may not have reflected the opinions of the average citizen. While Americans were disappointed by the actions of the White Sox players, it isn't clear that most people thought the players should go to prison or even be banished from the game. Indeed, fans across the country turned out in impressive numbers to watch the Black Sox players play

Six years after the Black Sox trial, Judge Landis was still trying to deal with rumors of fixed games in the major leagues. In this photograph, taken on January 5, 1927, Landis (*top left*) can be seen presiding over a hearing on a number of allegedly fixed games involving the White Sox and the Detroit Tigers. Charles Risberg, Buck Weaver, and Chick Gandil participated in the hearing. Joe Jackson and Eddie Cicotte declined the commissioner's invitation to appear.

in semipro and outlaw leagues (baseball leagues and games that were not sanctioned by major league baseball).

It seems odd, even hypocritical, that the state's quest for justice did not extend to Rothstein, Evans, and Attell, who were directly involved in the scheme. The same could be said for Comiskey, who, in trying to cover up the fix, may have obstructed justice. Moreover, the theft of the grand jury confessions was never investigated, even after the confessions turned up in the briefcase of one of Comiskey's lawyers during a civil suit that Weaver and Jackson brought against the White Sox owner several years later.

THE PLAYERS

Commissioner Landis's decision brought down the curtains on the professional careers of the Black Sox players. Despite the comparatively low pay that Comiskey gave them, their lives as ballplayers were preferable to the uncertain future that now faced them. For a pittance, they had given up a lifetime of unblemished glory. Now, their exclusion from the game drastically changed their lives. Most played in semiprofessional and outlaw leagues before settling into various occupations in maintenance, retail, and agriculture.

Despite his baseball exile, and years after his death, Joe Jackson remains a baseball legend. Jackson continues to be at the center of a debate about whether he should be inducted into baseball's Hall of Fame. Many of his supporters still claim that the slugger was treated unfairly by Commissioner Landis. Even those who agree that Jackson was actively involved in the fix have argued that his superior statistics should be enough to secure his place in the Hall of Fame.

Until he died in 1956, Buck Weaver (shown playing semipro ball for a Hammond, Indiana, team) made numerous unsuccessful appeals to be reinstated into major league baseball. His case is the most sympathetic of all the Black Sox players.

This photo, taken on October 3, 1939, shows Joe Jackson at the register in his liquor store in Greenville, South Carolina. Jackson played in semipro leagues, ran a dry-cleaning business, then a liquor store after he was banned from major league baseball. He maintained that he played the 1919 World Series on the level until he died in 1951.

THE GAME

Of course, over time, major league baseball overcame the Black Sox scandal. Between Landis's ironfisted rule over the game and Babe Ruth's remarkable home run exploits during the 1920s, the game quickly saw a return to the popularity it enjoyed in 1919. In time, the relationship between owners and players would change, and the oppressive reserve clause would give way to the current right to free agency, which is fiercely protected by a strong labor union—easily the most powerful in all of professional sports. The office of the commissioner remains a powerful force in the game, and the rules against gambling that Landis instituted are still rigidly enforced.

As of this writing, the Chicago White Sox have not won a World Series since the Black Sox scandal.

GLOSSARY

bill of particulars A detailed statement that outlines the charges against a defendant.

bookie A gambler who accepts and pays off bets.

conspire To secretly plan together to commit a crime.

defense The lawyer or team of lawyers who represents the defendant in a trial; the arguments presented by the defendant's legal representative.

defraud To cheat.

deliberate For a trial jury, to consider evidence and testimony before reaching a verdict.

fix The act of playing a game dishonestly to effect a particular outcome, usually a loss by the player or players involved.

free agency The status of a professional athlete having no contractual obligation to play for one team and the freedom to negotiate with any team.

grand jury A jury of between twelve and twenty-three persons that is assembled to investigate whether there is enough evidence with which to charge a suspect with a crime.

immunity Exemption from prosecution, penalty, or a legal duty.

inadmissible   Not allowed to be recognized. In a trial, inadmissible testimony or evidence cannot be considered by the jury.

indictment   The formal charge issued by a grand jury stating that there is enough evidence against the defendant to justify having a trial.

odds   The chances of winning a bet that is established by the bookie. It is a ratio that shows how much will be paid on a winning bet for each dollar wagered.

pennant   A flag that symbolizes the championship of a professional baseball league; the championship so symbolized.

prosecution   The government lawyer or team of lawyers who tries a criminal case, or presents evidence to show the guilt of the person or persons being tried; the act of trying a criminal case.

subpoena   A summons to appear in court.

syndicated   Having one's articles published in many newspapers or magazines at the same time or within a short period of time.

FOR MORE INFORMATION

Chicago Historical Society
Clark Street at North Avenue
Chicago, IL 60614-6071
(312) 642-4600
Web site: http://www.chicagohs.org

Chicago White Sox
333 West 35th Street
Chicago, IL 60616
(866) 769-4263
Web site: http://www.chisox.com

Major League Baseball
MLB Advanced Media
75 Ninth Avenue
New York, NY 10011
(866) 225-6457
Web site: http://www.mlb.com

National Baseball Hall of Fame and Museum
25 Main Street
P.O. Box 590
Cooperstown, NY 13326
(888) 425-5633
Web site: http://www.baseballhalloffame.org

WEB SITES

Due to the changing nature of Internet links, the Rosen Publishing Group, Inc., has developed an online list of Web sites related to the subject of this book. This site is updated regularly. Please use this link to access the list:

http://www.rosenlinks.com/gttc/cbst

FOR FURTHER READING

Asinof, Eliot. *Eight Men Out: The Black Sox and the 1919 World Series.*
New York: Owl Books, 1987.

Cook, William A. *The 1919 World Series: What Really Happened?*
Jefferson, NC: McFarland & Company, 2001.

Fleitz, David L. *Shoeless: The Life and Times of Joe Jackson.* Jefferson,
NC: McFarland & Company, 2001.

Lindberg, Richard C. *The White Sox Encyclopedia.* Philadelphia:
Temple University Press, 1997.

BIBLIOGRAPHY

APBNews.com. "Grand Jury Testimony of Joe Jackson." Retrieved
    August 2002 (http://www.apbnews.com/media/gfiles/shoelessjoe/
    docs.html).

Asinof, Eliot. *Eight Men Out: The Black Sox and the 1919 World Series.*
    New York: Owl Books, 1987.

The Chicago Historical Society. "The Black Sox." Retrieved August
    8, 2002 (http://www.chicagohs.org/history/blacksox.html).

Cook, William A. *The 1919 World Series: What Really Happened?*
    Jefferson, NC: McFarland & Company, 2001.

Fleitz, David L. *Shoeless: The Life and Times of Joe Jackson.* Jefferson,
    NC: McFarland & Company, 2001.

Lindberg, Richard C. *The White Sox Encyclopedia.* Philadelphia:
    Temple University Press, 1997.

Linder, Douglas. "The Black Sox Trial: An Account." University of
    Missouri Kansas City School of Law. Retrieved August 9, 2002
    (http://www.law.umkc.edu/faculty/projects/ftrials/blacksox/
    blacksoxaccount.html).

Ward, Geoffrey C., and Ken Burns. *Baseball: An Illustrated History.*
    New York: Alfred A. Knopf, 2001.

PRIMARY SOURCE IMAGE LIST

Cover: Photograph of members of the Chicago White Sox. Taken on September 16, 1919, in Chicago, Illinois.

Page 4: Photograph of crowds outside Redland Field. Taken in Cincinnati, Ohio, on October 1, 1919.

Page 8: At left, photograph of Chick Gandil, taken in Chicago in June 1921. At right, baseball card of Chick Gandil, created circa 1909–1911. Issued by the American Tobacco Company. From the Benjamin K. Edwards Collection, housed in the Library of Congress.

Page 9: Photograph of Eddie Cicotte. Taken on September 18, 1919, in Chicago, Illinois.

Page 10: Photo spread of the eight Black Sox from a 1920 article in *The Sporting News* newspaper.

Page 12: Photograph of Joe Jackson. Taken on May 25, 1920, in Chicago, Illinois.

Page 14: At left, photograph of Abe Attell. At right, photograph of Arnold Rothstein taken in the 1920s.

Page 17: Photograph of Kid Gleason. Taken in Chicago, Illinois.

Page 18: Photograph of Buck Weaver. Taken on Redland Field in Cincinnati, Ohio, on October 2, 1919. Housed in the Chicago Historical Society.

Page 21: Photograph of the Chicago White Sox playing field. Taken in Chicago, Illinois, in 1919.

Page 24: Photograph of Kid Gleason and Charles Comiskey. Taken by a *Chicago Daily News* photographer in Chicago, Illinois, in 1919. Housed in the Chicago Historical Society.

Page 26: Photograph of Governor John Tener, Garry Herrman, and Ban Johnson. Taken on January 25, 1915.

Page 27: Photograph of Hartley Repogle and Joe Jackson. Taken in September 1920 in Chicago, Illinois.

Page 28: Photograph of Oscar Felsch. Taken on October 29, 1917, in Chicago, Illinois.

Page 29: Cartoon about the Black Sox scandal. Created by John McCutcheon. Printed in the *Chicago Tribune* on September 24, 1920.

Page 30: Photographic portrait of Judge Kenesaw Mountain Landis. Taken by the Underwood and Underwood Agency.

Page 31: Photograph of Judge Kenesaw Mountain Landis and baseball franchise owners. Taken in 1920 in a courtroom in Chicago, Illinois, by a *Chicago Daily News* photographer. Housed in the Chicago Historical Society.

Page 34: Photograph of Chicago's Criminal Courts Building. Taken by Harold Allen on May 24, 1964.

Page 35: Photograph of Chick Gandil, Claude Williams, Charlie Risberg, Eddie Cicotte, Buck Weaver, Joe Jackson, Thomas Nash, James O'Brien, Max Luster, and two unidentified men. Taken in 1921 by a *Chicago Daily News* photographer. Housed in the Chicago Historical Society.

p.37: Photograph of Judge William Dever. Taken in a courtroom in Chicago, Illinois, in 1920 by a *Chicago Daily News* photographer. Housed in the Chicago Historical Society.

Page 40: Photograph of Judge Hugo Friend. Taken in Chicago, Illinois, on July 22, 1921.

Page 42: Photograph of Bill Burns. Taken by an Underwood and Underwood photographer on July 21, 1921.

Page 43: Photograph of George Gorman. Taken in 1925 in Chicago, Illinois, by a *Chicago Daily News* photographer. Housed in the Chicago Historical Society.

Page 46: Photograph of Benedict Short in 1928. Taken in Chicago, Illinois by a *Chicago Daily News* photographer. Housed in the Chicago Historical Society.

Page 50: Photograph of White Sox players. Taken in Chicago, Illinois, on January 5, 1927.

Page 51: Photograph of Buck Weaver. Taken in 1927 by a *Chicago Daily News* photographer. Housed in the Chicago Historical Society.

Page 52: Photograph of Joe Jackson. Taken on October 2, 1939, in Greenville, South Carolina.

INDEX

ABOUT THE AUTHOR

Wayne Anderson is a freelance writer and editor who lives in New York City. A native of Jamaica, he is a former music editor for the *New York Carib News*, the largest Caribbean American newsweekly in the United States, and he has written numerous entertainment feature articles in such magazines as *Elle*, *Emerge*, and *The Source*. He is an avid baseball fan who first became interested in the story of the Black Sox when he saw the movie *Field of Dreams* in 1989. Anderson is currently working on a collection of poems.

CREDITS

Cover, pp. 1, 4, 8 (left), 14, 22, 26, 27, 28, 29, 35, 39, 40, 50, 52 © Bettmann/Corbis; p. 2 Farm Security Administration, Office of War Information Photograph Collection, Library of Congress Prints and Photographs Division; p. 8 (right) the Benjamin K. Edwards Collection, Library of Congress Prints and Photographs Division; pp. 9, 12, 17, 30, 42 © Underwood & Underwood/Corbis; p. 10 Sporting News Archive; pp. 18, 24, 31, 35, 37, 43, 46, 51 Chicago Historical Society; p. 21 © Hulton/Archive/Getty Images; p. 29 © Corbis; p. 34 Historic American Buildings Survey, Library of Congress Prints and Photographs Division.

Designer: Les Kanturek; **Editor:** Christine Poolos

First American edition, 1990.
Text copyright © 1990 by Terence Blacker. Illustrations copyright © 1990 by Pippa Unwin.
All rights reserved under International and Pan-American Copyright Conventions.
Published in the United States by Random House, Inc., New York.
Published in Great Britain by Andersen Press Ltd., London.
Published in Australia by Century Hutchinson Australia Pty., Ltd., Sydney.

Library of Congress Cataloging-in-Publication Data
Blacker, Terence.
Herbie Hamster, where are you?
Summary: When Danny goes to feed his pet hamster he finds the cage empty and no sign of his pet.
The reader can help Danny look for his hamster in each illustration.
[1. Hamsters—Fiction] I. Unwin, Pippa, ill. II. Title.
PZ7.B53225.He 1990 [E] 90-8053
ISBN 0-679-80838-8

Printed in Italy by Grafiche AZ, Verona. 1 2 3 4 5 6 7 8 9 10

Herbie Hamster, Where Are You?

by Terence Blacker

illustrated by Pippa Unwin

Random House 🏠 New York

It's time for Danny to feed Herbie Hamster.
Uh-oh! He's not in his cage!

Danny better find him.
Herbie Hamster, where are you?

Herbie might be visiting the neighbors.
The family next door is having a delicious snack.

Herbie Hamster's always ready for a snack.
He must be here. But where?

Maybe Herbie went on to Miss Frumble's house.
Miss Frumble likes cats.

And cats…like hamsters!
Herbie better watch out!

The twins down the block are having
a birthday party!

Did Herbie invite himself?
He's there…somewhere.

Wow! Look at all those toys!
Herbie would love playing at the Wrights' house.

He must have stopped by there.
Herbie Hamster, where are you?

David is painting a picture of Peter
playing the piano.

Herbie likes music. He must have a good seat.
Where's Herbie?

The Greens don't seem to be home.
But their dogs are!

What a hullabaloo!
Herbie Hamster, are you having fun?

Mr. Talbot must have been asleep.
Probably the doorbell woke him.

Danny sees himself in the mirror.
But he doesn't see Herbie. Keep looking!

Miss Peachum, in the house on the corner,
sees something small and furry.

"Help!" she screams. She jumps out of the tub.
 Where's Herbie?

"Help! A rat!" hollers Miss Peachum.
All the neighbors rush outside.

It's not a rat.
It's Herbie Hamster!

Mommy hears the doorbell.
"Herbie Hamster's home at last," says Danny.

"Where has he been?" asks Mommy.
"Everywhere!" Danny answers.